Easy
Animal
Mazes

by
Anna Pomaska
and Suzanne Ross

DOVER PUBLICATIO

D0150230

Published in Canada by General Publishing Company,
Ltd., 30 Lesmill Road, Don Mills, Toronto, Ontario.
Published in the United Kingdom by Constable and
Company, Ltd.

Easy Animal Mazes is a new work, first published by
Dover Publications, Inc., in 1990.

International Standard Book Number: 0-486-26282-0

Manufactured in the United States of America
Dover Publications, Inc., 31 East 2nd Street, Mineola,
N.Y. 11501

Note

Inside the pages of this book
are charming animals, who look
for special places, things to eat,
or playmates they've arranged to meet.
Each eager creature, as you'll find,
can't reach the goal it has in mind
unless you guide it on its ways
through all the windings of a maze.
Along the path, you must beware
of pitfalls stationed here and there;
or, if your journey's trouble-free,
there may be things to stop and see,
not to mention some precious find
that your companion won't leave behind.
No puzzle here is hard to solve
if you have courage and resolve—
but if you and your animal friend
get lost before the maze's end,
just turn to the Solutions section*
and you will see the whole connection!

*Page 51.

Pup wants to end his long balloon flight,
and land near his friend who is in sight.

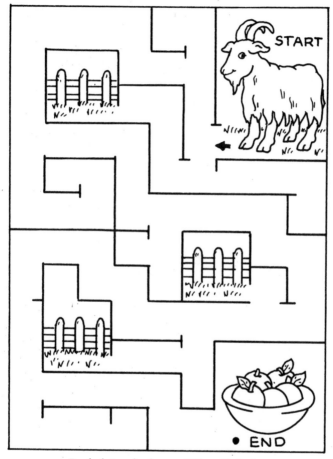

By dodging the fences, Billy will find
the bowl of apples that's on his mind.

5

START

END

Bridget the bird wants to find her nest,
while avoiding the homes of all the rest.

On coral this fishy would love to feed,
without being caught in waving seaweed.

7

END

START

Beaver, who's building a dam on this site,
must bring one last stick, to make it just right!

Flash the pig wants to soar with his friend,
Captain Leeward, at Maze's End.

Pinto the filly is galloping fast;
help her get to the barn at last.

Pegasus, the winged horse, will be forlorn
if he can't fly down to the unicorn.

Panda must pick up only bamboo,
then reach the big bunch for his dinner too.

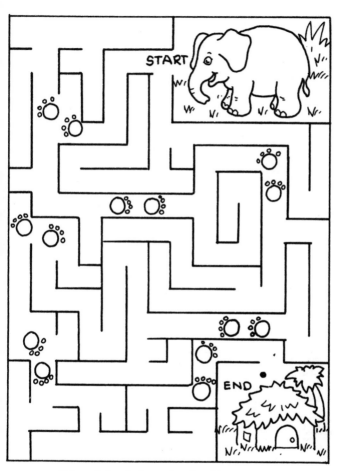

START

END

Edward the elephant, here's a hint:
get home by following your own footprint!

13

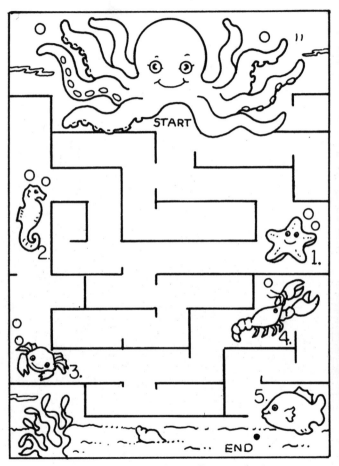

START

2.

1.

4.

3.

5.

END

Octopus goes to the sea floor to play,
picking up all five friends on the way.

"Which rocky path," asks Snake with a groan,
"will lead me back to my home in the stone?"

Dachsie brings creatures whose names start with D
along to his doghouse for date pie and tea.

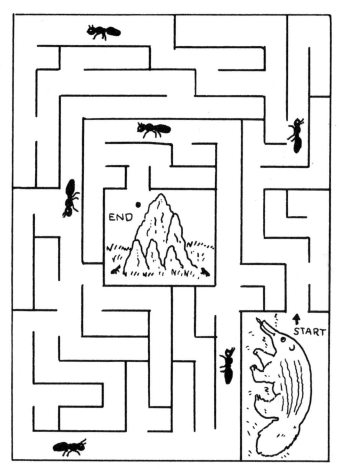

Help Anteater find what he likes the best.
By following the ants, he'll reach their nest.

17

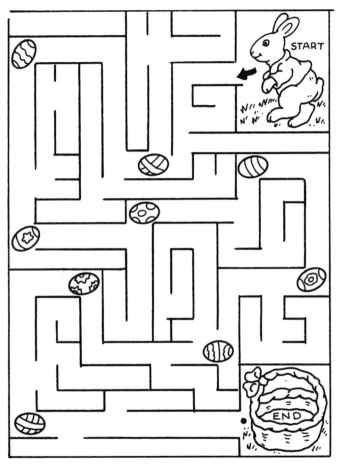

Nine Easter eggs—what wonderful fun!
They must fill Bunny's basket when journey's done.

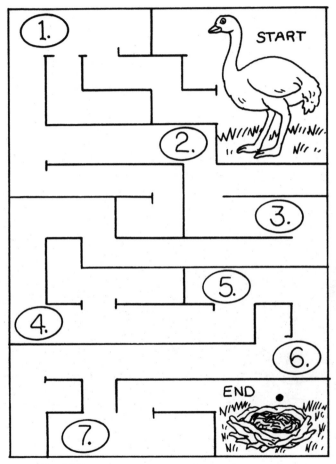

Ostrich has seven eggs scattered around.
Her nest will hold all of them when they are found.

19

Frieda the frog wants to see her friend Friz.
She must hop on two lilypads—then she'll reach his!

Ma Kangaroo sees a place for a drink.
Can you get her there in ten hops, do you think?

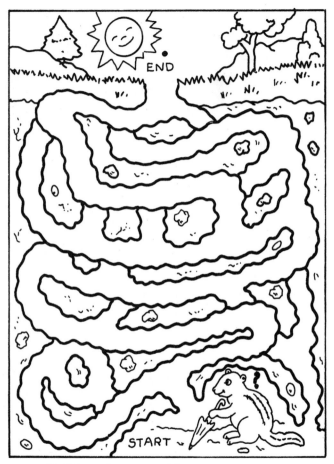

If Chipmunk goes up without any stop,
will he need that umbrella when reaching the top?

START

END

Help poor Daddy Raccoon to see
whether his baby's safe in the tree.

23

Through nine banana circles Monkey must roam
and touch no blank circles—then he'll get home!

START

END

Won't you be Miss Kitty's friend?
Help find her milk jug at the end.

25

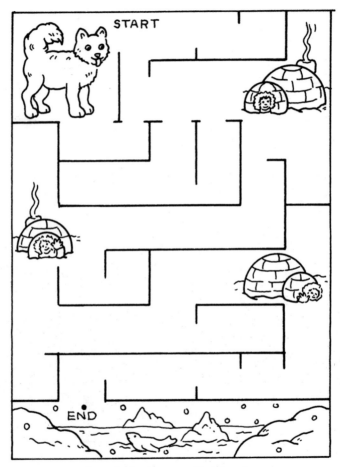

Ikwa the husky meets Seal for play,
fetching all children along the way.

START

END

Rudolph must get to the houses below.
It's Christmas Eve, and he can't be slow!

27

Triceratops wants to visit his friend,
Brontosaurus, at this maze's end.

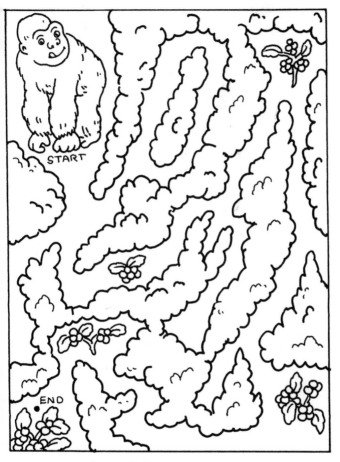

Is this gorilla hungry? Very!
That's why he must collect every berry!

29

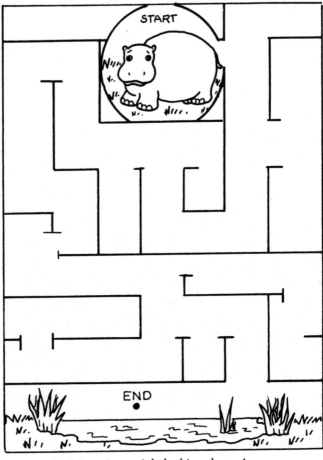

Hippo is certainly looking gloomy!
He needs a muddy place that is roomy.

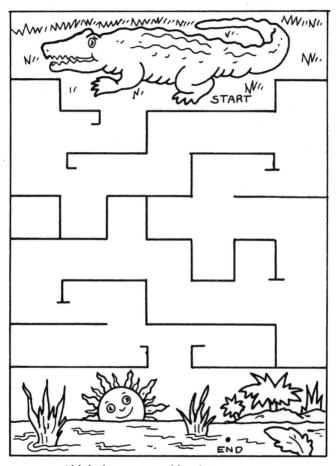

START

END

Al left the swamp and lost his way.
Help him get home by the end of the day!

END

START

Mama Kitty feels it is best
to return to her little ones after her rest.

Fox would like to go fishing today,
if he can avoid the skunks on the way!

33

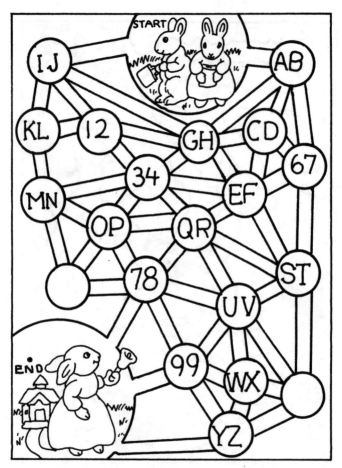

These bunnies learned the alphabet well.
They can follow it down to their teacher's bell!

34

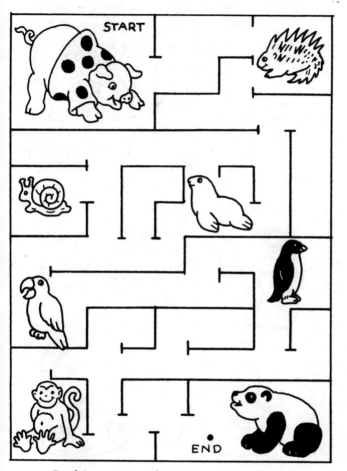

Panda's a creature whom Pig wants to see,
and so are the others whose names start with P.

Sorrel, that squirrel with the basket, must try
to gather six acorns for scrumptious Nut Pie!

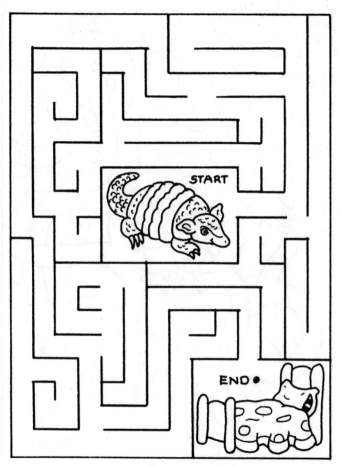

Help this sleepy armadillo
find his comfy bed and pillow.

Myron the mouse wants to see Mary Lou,
but he must stay clear of You-Know-Whooo!

These dolphins like swimming beside their friend,
who sails a boat at this maze's end.

39

Honeybee has nectar to take to her hive.
Won't you please help her safely arrive?

Ginny Giraffe is invited to lunch.
When she meets her friend, on leaves they will much!

This hungry mouse will be full of bliss
when he reaches that very big wedge of Swiss.

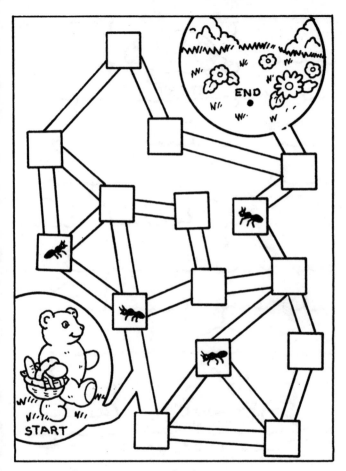

Ted wants to picnic in his favorite space,
but stay clear of ants on the way to that place.

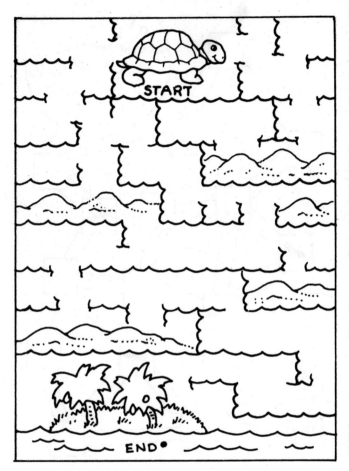

If Thurston the turtle avoids each sand dune,
he'll get to the island in the lagoon.

If Camel hits no cactus while passing by,
he'll reach the oasis, and not be so dry.

45

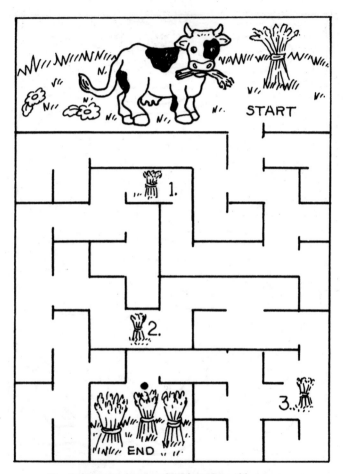

Bessie knows where to find bunches of hay—
but still wants to nibble three times on her way.

With a lot of your help and a little luck,
Downie will join up with Mama Duck.

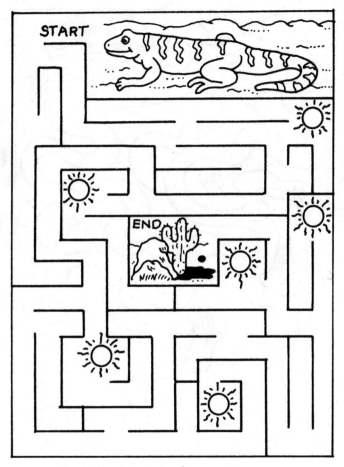

In the hot desert, Lizard must scurry
to avoid the sun and find shade in a hurry!

Collect 12 stripes, touch no blank space,
And Horse will be Zebra on ending the race!

49

page 4

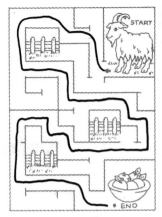

page 5

page 6

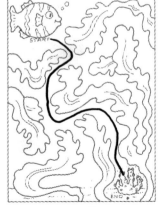

page 7

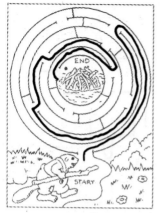

page 8

page 9

page 10

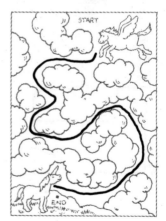

page 11

page 12

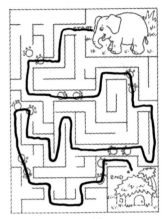

page 13

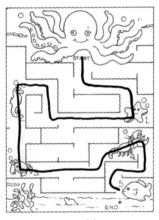

page 14

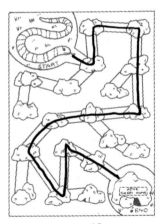

page 15

page 16

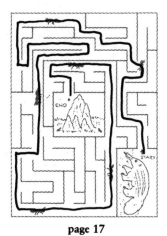

page 17

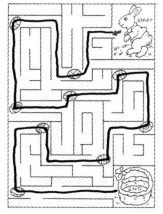

page 18

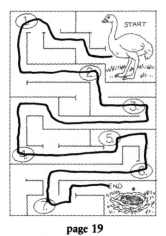

page 19

page 20

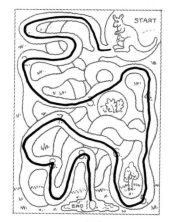

page 21

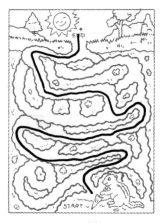

page 22

page 23

56

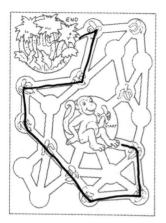

page 24

page 25

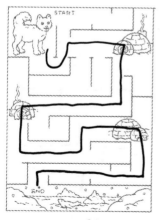

page 26

page 27

page 28

page 29

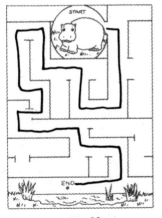

page 30

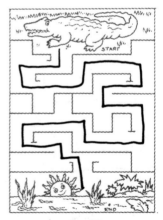

page 31

page 32

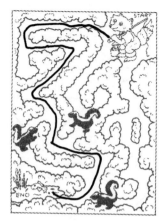

page 33

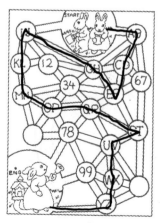

page 34

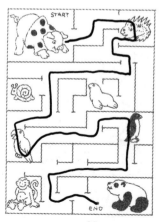

page 35

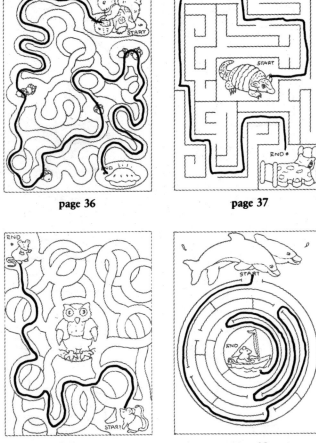

page 36

page 37

page 38

page 39

page 40

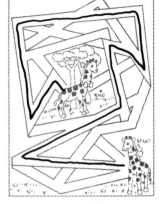

page 41

page 42

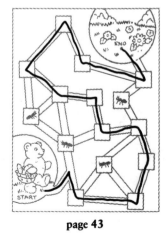

page 43

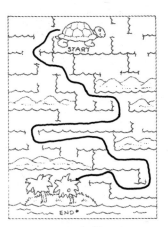

page 44

page 45

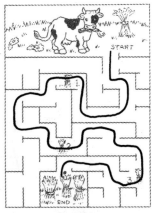

page 46

page 47